Light and colour

Contents

Teachers' notes	1
Day and night	5
Light and shadows	6
Make your own shadows	7
Shadow shapes	8
Shadow matching	9
How many shadows?	10
A shadow clock	11
Eyes	12
Why do we have two eyes?	13
Can we always believe our eyes?	14
Blindness	15
What can you see through?	16
Letting light pass through	17
Mixing colours	18
Spinning colours	19
Changing colours	20
Unmixing colours	21
Rainbows	22
Shiny things	23
Reflections	24
Pictures in the mirror	25
Mirror tricks	26
Reflecting sunlight	27
Bending light	28
Magnifying glasses	29
Make a magnifier	30
Animals in the light and dark	31
Plants and light	32

Teachers' notes

Aims of this book

• To show that our light during the day comes mainly from the Sun, while at night we rely largely on artificial lights.
• To show that to cause a shadow you need light and an object that blocks the light.
• To show that materials can be classified as opaque, transparent or translucent.
• To show that light can be reflected.
• To demonstrate the effects of mirrors and magnifying glasses.
• To name some colours and to show what happens when they are mixed.

Developing science skills

While it is not essential to follow the order of the worksheets in this book, it is important that all those covering one aspect of the subject are dealt with at approximately the same time.

Although it is in the *doing* of science that children learn best, this involves more than just practical work. They need to observe, record, predict, measure, look for patterns, classify, explain and ask questions that can lead to further investigations. They need time to discuss their work, before and after the activity: this will also aid the teacher in monitoring the children's progress so that they build a valid framework for future development.

Safety precautions

When teaching children about light they should be warned not to look directly at the Sun, its reflection, or bright artificial lights. Also, use plastic mirrors and lenses where possible. If unframed glass mirrors have to be used, tape the edges and stick a cross of tape on the back to reduce the risk of splinters if the mirror is broken.

Scientific background

This information is intended to help you understand the scientific concepts and ideas covered in this book. It generally goes beyond the level of understanding expected of most children, but it will give you the confidence to ask and answer questions and to guide the children in their investigations. Further information is contained in the worksheet notes.

Light

Light is a form of radiation to which the human eye is sensitive. Without light we cannot see. The Sun, stars, electric lights and flames all give out light; they are luminous. Some clocks and watches, and a few plants and animals are able to produce light from chemicals. All other objects we see reflect the light that falls on them.

Light travels in waves which move in straight lines. It cannot go round corners. If light meets an object through which it cannot pass, a shadow of that object is produced.

Colours

White light consists of a mixture of several colours of light. Objects which do not give out light appear coloured because they reflect certain colours of light falling on them. A red car

▲ ESSENTIALS FOR SCIENCE: Light and colour

1

appears red because it reflects red and absorbs the rest of the spectrum.

Reflection and refraction
When light can easily pass through materials, they are said to be *transparent*. *Translucent* materials allow light to pass through them, but do not allow us to see through them clearly. Other materials which absorb or reflect the light falling on them are said to be *opaque*. A completely black surface absorbs all light falling on it, while highly-polished surfaces *reflect* the light in one direction. These act as mirrors.

Light travels through different materials at different speeds. It travels faster through air than through water. That is why a spoon which is half submerged in a tumbler of water, appears to be bent. The direction in which the light is travelling changes at the point where the spoon enters the water. This is called *refraction*.

Notes on individual activities

Page 5: Day and night
Key ideas: the Sun gives light during the day. At night we use electric lights, although we get some light from the stars and, reflected from the Sun, from the Moon.
Extension activity: discuss the advantages and disadvantages of different kinds of artificial lights.

Page 6: Light and shadows
Key idea: even dim lights form a visible shadow of an opaque object in a darkened room.
Likely outcome: if the room is dark enough, all of the lights will form a shadow. It may be necessary to vary the distance between the light and the wall to produce a distinct shadow. The best shadow is produced by the brightest light.
Extension activity: experiment to find out whether coloured lights form coloured shadows.

Page 7: Make your own shadows
Key idea: shadows are the approximate shape of the objects forming them.
Extension activity: discuss why transparent objects do not form shadows.

Page 8: Shadow shapes
Key ideas: the angle and direction of light falling on an object affect the size and shape of the shadow. Transparent objects do not form shadows.
Likely outcome: when the light is coming from the right, a long shadow will be formed on the left of the object; when the light is coming from the left, a long shadow will be formed on the right; and when the light is coming from above, the shadow will be very small. If the beaker is completely transparent it will not form a shadow.
Extension activity: demonstrate the changing length and position of a shadow when a light is moved through 180°. This will help children to understand the way shadows change as the Earth orbits the Sun.

Page 9: Shadow matching
Key idea: a shadow is the approximate shape of the illuminated object which formed it.
Extension activity: discuss the use of silhouettes in, for example, road signs.

Page 10: How many shadows?
Key idea: two or more shadows of an object can be made if two or more lights illuminate it.
Likely outcome: two torches will make two paler shadows. Three torches would produce three shadows. The shadows can be made longer by moving the torches further away from the object and shorter by moving them nearer to or holding them above the object.

Page 11: A shadow clock
Key idea: the length and position of shadows change as the Earth orbits the Sun.
Likely outcome: the length and position of the stick's shadow will change each hour. It will be shortest around midday when the Sun is directly overhead. The stick's shadow could be used to tell the time on a sunny day.
Extension activities: can a shadow created by an artificial light be used to tell the time? (No.)
Safety precautions: warn the children not to look directly at the Sun or at bright artificial lights.

Page 12: Eyes
Key ideas: our eyes alter according to how bright or dim the light is.
Likely outcome: the colour of the iris varies from person to person. The pupil of the eye is a hole which allows light into the sensitive rear part of the eye, the retina. The size of the opening is controlled by the iris. In dim light the pupil dilates to allow the maximum amount of light into the eye. In bright light the pupil narrows to reduce the amount of light entering the eye.
Extension activities: compare the eyes of dogs, cats and other pets with human eyes.
Safety precautions: warn the children not to look directly at the Sun or at bright artificial lights.

Page 13: Why do we have two eyes?
Key idea: having two eyes enables us to judge distances better.
Likely outcome: it is easier to touch the dot with the pencil point if both eyes are open.
Extension activities: try to throw a ball at a target,

▲ ESSENTIALS FOR SCIENCE: Light and colour

first with only one eye open and then with both eyes open. Which is the most accurate?

Page 14: Can we always believe our eyes?
Key idea: our eyes can sometimes deceive us.
Likely outcome: the fish will appear to be in the bowl. This activity demonstrates 'persistence of vision' – the brain retains an image for a fraction of a second after the event has occurred.
Extension activity: look at coloured objects under fluorescent lights and then outside in sunlight. Do the colours always appear the same?

Page 15: Blindness
Key ideas: sight is the sense we depend upon most. Blind people rely on other senses for information about what is going on around them.
Extension activity: find out more about guide dogs for the blind and how they are trained.

Page 16: What can you see through?
Key idea: some materials are transparent, some are opaque and some are translucent.
Likely outcome: opaque objects do not allow any light to pass through them. Transparent objects allow light to pass through so that it is possible to see through them clearly. Translucent objects allow a little light to pass through, but it is not possible to see through them clearly.
Extension activities: test opaque, transparent and translucent objects with a torch in a darkened room. Which make the best shadows? Compare liquids, such as water and milk, to see whether light can pass through them.

Page 17: Letting light pass through
Key idea: whether or not a material is transparent depends upon its thickness.
Likely outcome: as more layers of polythene are used, the material will cease to be transparent and will become translucent. Eventually, with enough layers, it will become opaque.
Extension activity: shine a torch through increasing numbers of coloured sheets of transparent plastic. Is the same result obtained?

Page 18: Mixing colours
Key ideas: different colours can be mixed to make new colours.
Likely outcome: yellow and red produce orange; blue and yellow produce green; blue and red make purple.
Extension activity: paint pictures using only the three primary colours, red, yellow and blue, but form new colours by mixing them.

Page 19: Spinning colours
Key idea: if colours are rotated rapidly, they appear to mix together and make new colours.
Likely outcome: the colours will appear to have been mixed, thus the red and yellow will appear orange, while red and blue will appear purple.
Extension activity: do this experiment again with different-sized tops. Which one works best?

Page 20: Changing colours
Key idea: the colours of some objects appear to change when viewed through coloured filters.
Likely outcome: a red filter will remove the other colours from light so that objects look mostly red.
Extension activities: use a coloured filter with a torch. What colour do objects appear to be?

Page 21: Unmixing colours
Key idea: some everyday coloured substances are, in reality, mixtures of colours.
Likely outcome: if water-based felt-tipped pens are used, some of the colours will separate out into distinct bands showing that they were composed of mixtures of colours.
Extension activities: try to separate out the colours of various fruit drinks using this technique.

Page 22: Rainbows
Key idea: a rainbow consists of bands of colour produced when raindrops split up sunlight into its constituent colours.
Likely outcome: the colours of the rainbow are, from top to bottom, red, orange, yellow, green, blue, indigo and violet. Rainbows may also appear in oily puddles, soap bubbles, and near fountains and waterfalls in sunny weather.
Extension activity: use a prism to split the light from a torch into its constituent colours.

Page 23: Shiny things
Key idea: some objects and materials reflect a great deal of light and are described as shiny.
Likely outcome: polished metal objects are the shiniest. Objects or materials with a rough or uneven surface are least shiny.
Extension activity: use metal polish to increase the shininess of a piece of metal.

Page 24: Reflections
Key idea: light is reflected by shiny objects. Curved reflections produce a distorted image.
Likely outcome: the image produced in the bowl of the spoon will be quite large and upside down. The image in the back of the spoon is smaller and the right way up.

Page 25: Pictures in the mirror
Key idea: a mirror can be used to complete a picture which has symmetry.
Extension activities: use a mirror to investigate the symmetry of frontal photographs of faces. Do both sides produce slightly different people?

Page 26: Mirror tricks

Key idea: by using two mirrors it is possible to produce reflections of reflections.
Likely outcome: with care it will be possible to see multiple reflections (reflections of reflections).
Extension activity: look for reflections in unusual places – in puddles, in the sides of tins and so on.

Page 27: Reflecting sunlight

Key idea: a mirror has a highly reflective surface and will reflect sunlight.
Likely outcome: a small patch of sunlight can be focused on the wall. With care, it can be reflected round a corner if the person holding the mirror stands near the angle of the corner.
Extension activity: which other shiny surfaces will reflect the Sun's light on to a wall?
Safety precautions: use plastic mirrors if possible. The children should not reflect the sunlight into people's eyes or on to paper or fabric.

Page 28: Bending light

Key idea: light is bent when it passes from air into water; it travels more slowly in water than in air.
Likely outcome: viewed from the side, the straw appears bent. Looked at from above it appears to be straight. The same happens with a ruler.

Page 29: Magnifying glasses

Key idea: a magnifying glass is a *convex* lens.
Likely outcome: the magnifying glass has to be held a little way above the object to obtain a sharp, magnified image.
Extension activity: use a magnifying glass to examine flowers, insects, stamps, CDs, salt and sugar and so on.

Page 30: Make a magnifier

Key idea: a drop or jar of water will focus light and act as a magnifying glass or lens.
Likely outcome: the drop, or jar of water when held horizontally, will act as a magnifying glass.
Extension activity: use a transparent cylindrical tube of water as a magnifier. Compare its power when filled with a clear vegetable oil.

Page 31: Animals in the light and dark

Key idea: many small nocturnal animals avoid the light.
Likely outcome: the woodlice or earthworms will usually congregate in the dark area.
Extension activity: find out about owls, bats and other animals which are mainly active at night.
Safety precautions: release the earthworms and woodlice in a suitable area as soon as possible.

Page 32: Plants and light

Key idea: plants need light if they are to be green.
Likely outcome: the seedlings grown in the dark will be tall, straggly and yellow. The ones grown in the light will be shorter, stouter and green. If the seedlings from the dark are put in the light place they will gradually turn green.
Extension activity: try this experiment with other kinds of seeds such as peas, beans, wheat, oats and barley. Do they produce the same result?

National Curriculum: Science

In addition to the PoS for AT1, the following PoS are relevant to this book:

AT2 Pupils should:
- find out about themselves and develop their ideas about how they grow, feed, move, use their senses and about the stages of human development.
- consider similarities and differences between themselves and other pupils and understand that individuals are unique.
- investigate what plants need to grow and reproduce.

AT3 Pupils should:
- collect and find similarities and differences between a variety of everyday materials.

AT4 Pupils should:
- have opportunities to explore light sources and the effects related to shadow, reflection and colour.
- observe closely the local natural environment to detect seasonal changes, including length of daylight...

Scottish 5 – 14 Curriculum: Environmental studies

Attainment outcome	Strand
Science in the environment	Living things; processes of life; energy; planet Earth.
Healthy and safe living	Looking after myself
Investigating	Planning; Finding out; Recording; Interpreting; Reporting
Designing and making	Planning; Making; Evaluating; Presenting

▲ ESSENTIALS FOR SCIENCE: Light and colour

▲ Name _____

Day and night

You will need: a pencil; coloured pencils or crayons.

This picture is of daytime.

▲ Draw the same place at night.

▲ Say how it is different.

▲ Colour both pictures.

▲ How many things can you think of which give out light?

▲ ESSENTIALS FOR SCIENCE: Light and colour

▲ Name _____

Light and shadows

You will need: a pencil; two or three different torches; a desk lamp; a table lamp; a doll.

Work in a darkened room. Ask an adult to help you.

▲ Lay one of the torches on a table. Switch it on. Point it at the wall.

▲ Move the doll between the torch and the wall so that you can you make a shadow of the doll.

▲ Now try the other lights.
- Do they all make a shadow?
- Which makes the best shadow?

▲ ESSENTIALS FOR SCIENCE: Light and colour

▲ Name _____

Make your own shadows

You will need: a pencil; a teapot; a cup and saucer; a shoe; a potted plant; a coffee mug; a plastic bottle; a torch.

▲ Look at the objects below. Draw the shadows you think they will make.

▲ Work in a dark corner. Shine your torch on the objects, one at a time to see if you are right.

▲ ESSENTIALS FOR SCIENCE: Light and colour

▲ Name

Shadow shapes

You will need: a torch; a pencil; a toy figure; a clear plastic beaker.
Work in a dark corner.

▲ Shine the torch on the figure in the directions shown below.
▲ Draw the shadow that is formed.

Directly from above

From the left

From the right

▲ Does a beaker make shadows in the same way?

▲ ESSENTIALS FOR SCIENCE: Light and colour

▲ Name _____

Shadow matching

You will need: a pencil; a ruler.

▲ Look carefully at the pictures below.

▲ Draw a line to join each picture to its shadow.

▲ Draw some shadow shapes of your own.

▲ ESSENTIALS FOR SCIENCE: Light and colour

▲ Name _____

How many shadows?

You will need: a pencil; two torches; a toy figure.
Work in a darkened room.

▲ Shine your torch on the figure. How many shadows do you see?

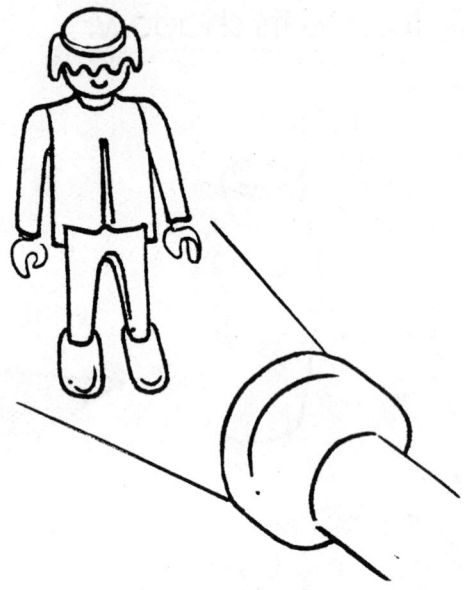

▲ Now shine two torches as shown in the picture below.
  • How many shadows do you see?
  • Are the shadows darker or paler than before?

▲ How could you make three shadows?

▲ How could you make the shadows longer or shorter?

▲ ESSENTIALS FOR SCIENCE: Light and colour

▲ Name _____

A shadow clock

You will need: a plastic bottle; sand or soil; a short stick; some pebbles.

Do this activity on a sunny morning. Do not look directly at the Sun.

▲ Fill the bottle with sand or soil. Push the stick in the top.

▲ Take the bottle into the playground and leave it there.

▲ Does the stick make a shadow? If so, mark the end of it with a pebble.

▲ Do this every hour.

▲ Does the shadow move? Why is this?

▲ Can you use the shadow to tell the time?

▲ ESSENTIALS FOR SCIENCE: Light and colour

▲ Name _____

Eyes

You will need: a pencil; a small mirror.
Work with a friend.

We see with our eyes. Without light we cannot see.

▲ Look at your eyes in the mirror. Can you see the same parts shown in the picture below?

▲ Colour the picture.

▲ Look at your friend's eyes. Are they same colour as yours?

▲ Ask your friend to look towards a bright light. Do **not** look at the Sun. What happens to the pupils of your friend's eyes?

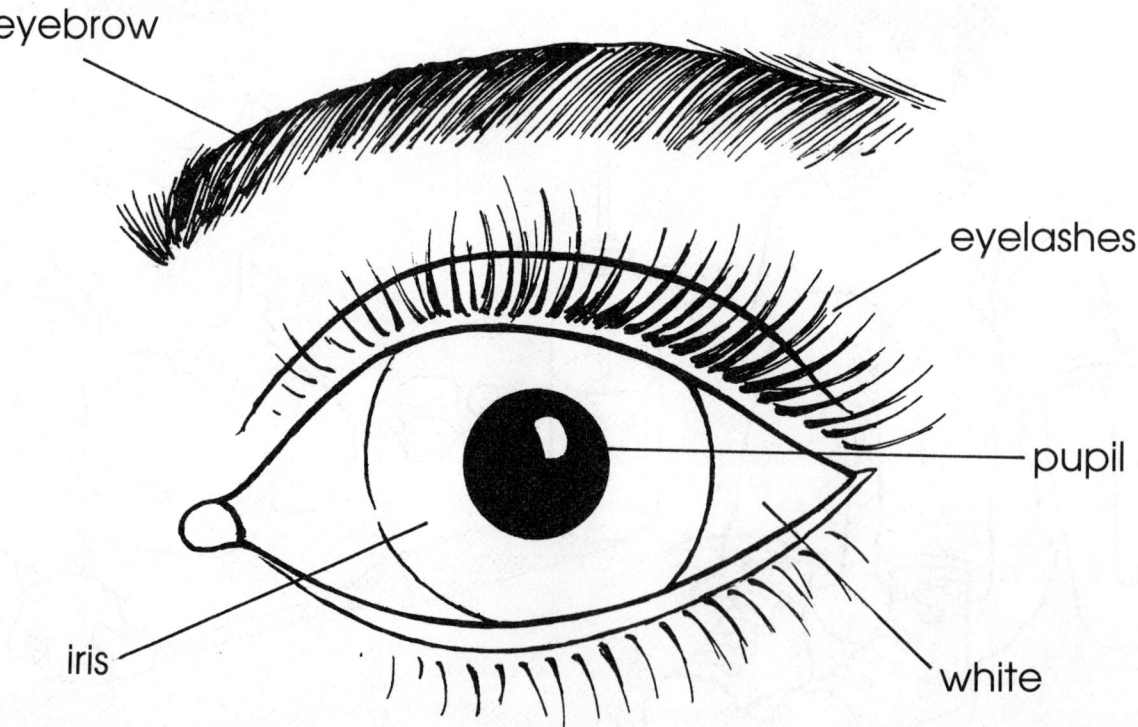

▲ Ask your friend to look into a dark corner. What happens to your friend's pupils now?

▲ Name _____

Why do we have two eyes?

You will need: a pencil; a piece of paper.

▲ Lay this sheet on the table in front of you.

▲ Cover one eye with your hand.

▲ Hold the pencil high in your other hand.

▲ Try to touch the dot *quickly* with the pencil.
  • Now try it with the other eye and hand.
  • Now try with both eyes open.
  • Which is easier?

●

▲ ESSENTIALS FOR SCIENCE: Light and colour

▲ Name _____

Can we always believe our eyes?

You will need: a piece of card; a short round stick or cane; a pencil.

▲ Ask an adult to split the top of the stick for you.

▲ Copy or trace the picture of a fish on to one side of a piece of card.

▲ Copy or trace the bowl on to the other side of the card.

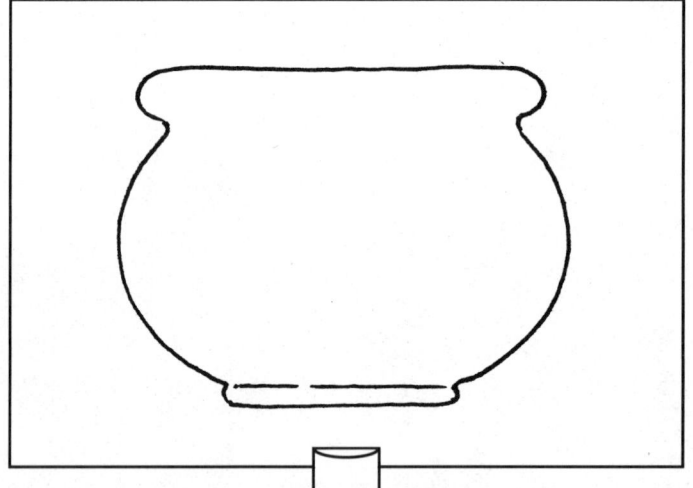

▲ Fix the card in the top of the stick.

▲ Spin the stick and the card. What do you see?

▲ Can you make a bird look as if it is in a cage?

▲ ESSENTIALS FOR SCIENCE: Light and colour

▲ Name _____

Blindness

You will need: a pencil; paper; a scarf.
Work with a friend.

People who cannot see are blind.

▲ What do you think it would be like to be blind?

▲ Ask your friend to tie a scarf around your eyes. Try to write or draw while your eyes are covered.

▲ Ask your friend to carefully lead you round the classroom. How do you feel?

▲ Find out how blind people are able to read. How are they able to find their way along busy streets?

_____
_____
_____
_____
_____
_____
_____

▲ ESSENTIALS FOR SCIENCE: Light and colour

▲ Name _____

What can you see through?

You will need: a pencil.

▲ Look around your classroom.
  • Which objects can you see through?
These are transparent.
  • Which objects can you almost see through?
These are translucent.
  • Which objects can you not see through?
These are opaque.

▲ Record your findings below.

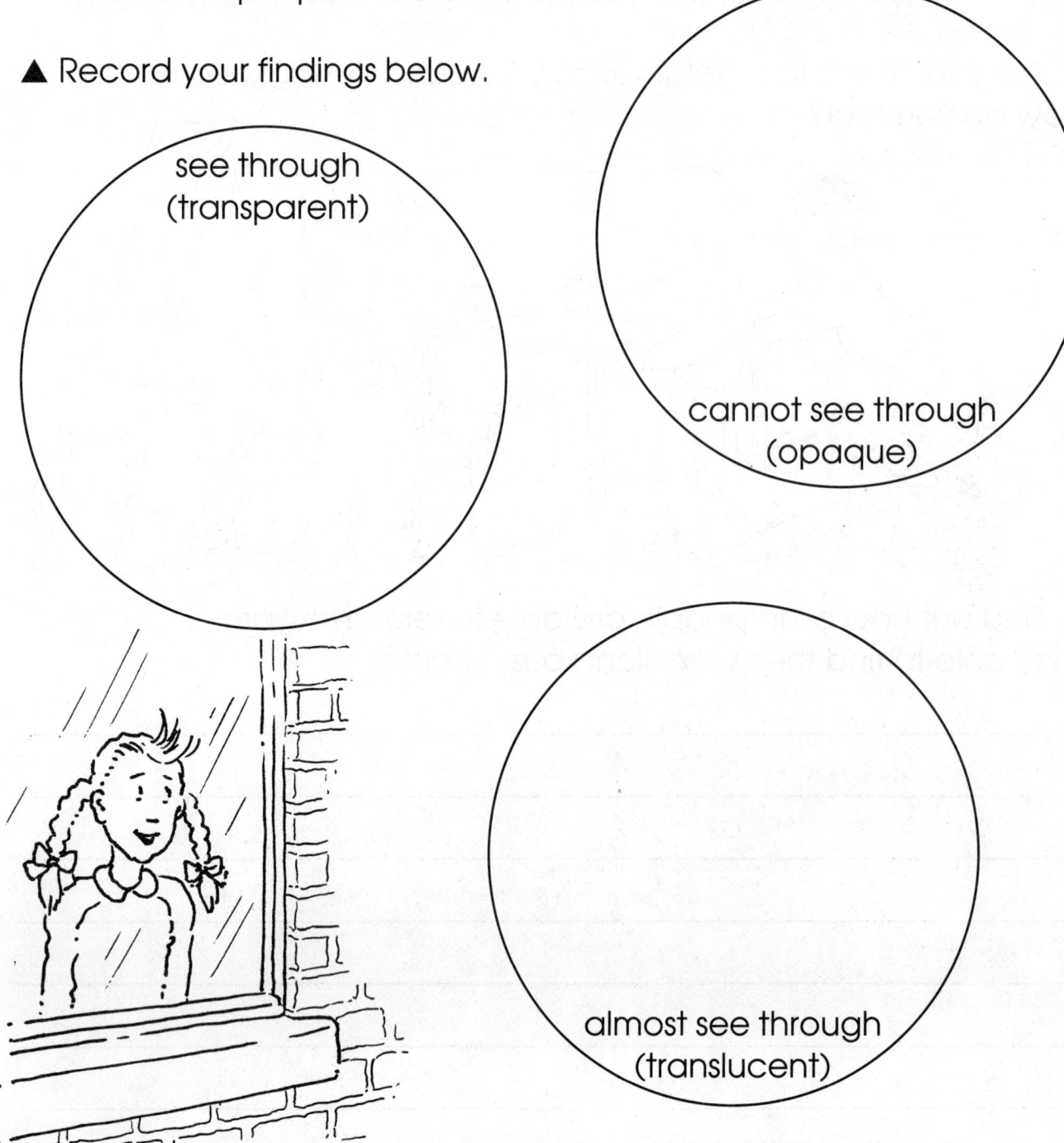

ESSENTIALS FOR SCIENCE: Light and colour

▲ Name _____

Letting light pass through

You will need: a coloured picture; some sheets of polythene; a pencil.

▲ Fix the picture on the wall.

▲ Hold a sheet of polythene in front of it. Can you still see the picture? If you can, the polythene is transparent.

▲ Now hold two sheets of polythene in front of the picture. Can you still see the picture?

▲ How many sheets of polythene must there be before you cannot see the picture?

▲ What have you learned about polythene?

▲ Find other materials which behave like this.

▲ ESSENTIALS FOR SCIENCE: Light and colour

▲ Name _____

Mixing colours

You will need: a pencil; some paints; a brush; some sheets of paper.

▲ Mix together the paints as shown by each circle.

▲ Paint them in the circles.
Say what colours you have made.

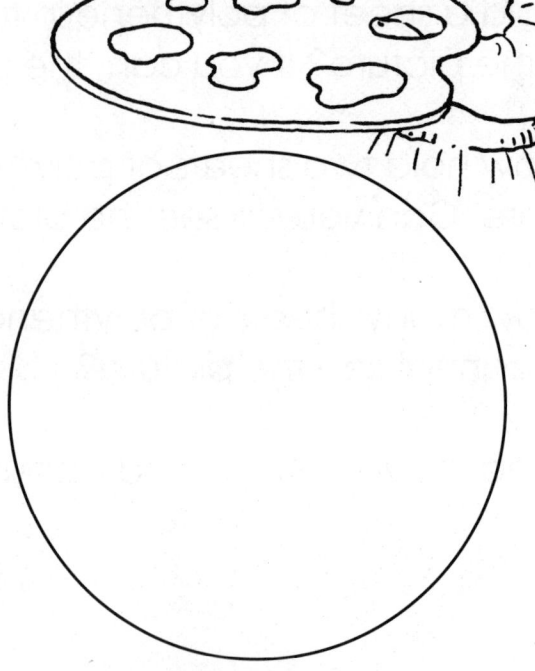

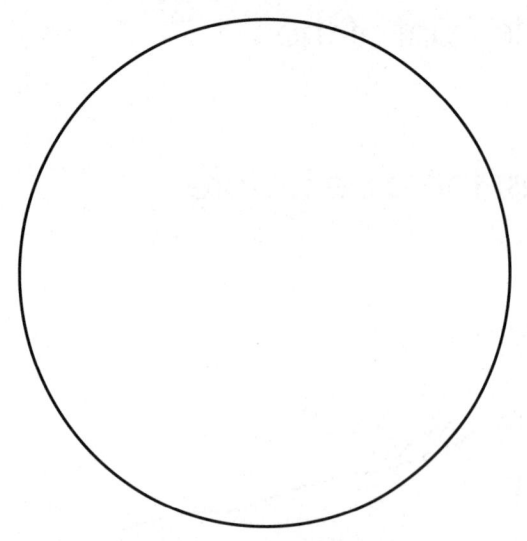

Red + yellow   **Blue + yellow**

_____   _____

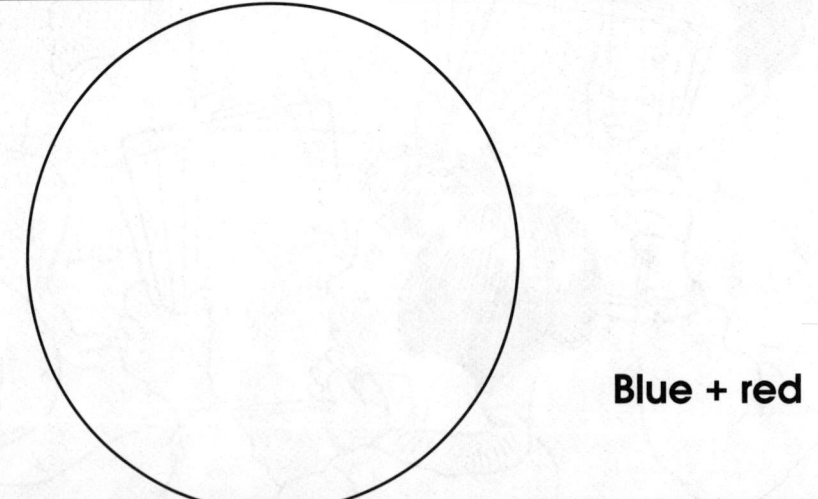

Blue + red

_____

▲ Try mixing other colours.
 • Can you invent a colour of your own?
 • Say how you made it.

▲ ESSENTIALS FOR SCIENCE: Light and colour

▲ Name _____

Spinning colours

You will need: a short piece of pencil; thin card; a small jar lid; paints or crayons.

▲ Use the lid to draw a small circle on a piece of card.

▲ Make a small hole in the centre of the circle.

▲ Colour the circle red and yellow as shown below.

▲ Push the piece of pencil through the hole to make a spinning top.

▲ Spin your top. What colour does it look?

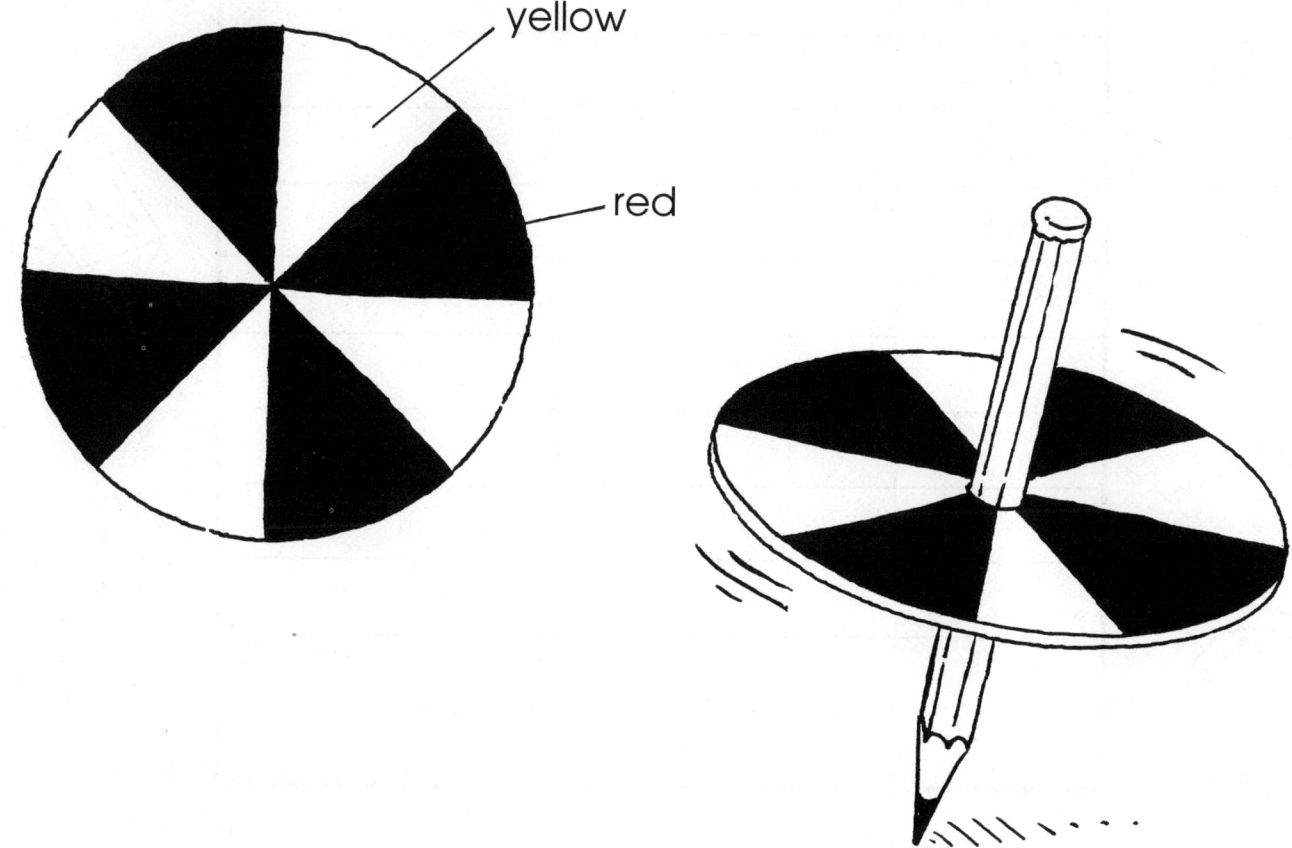

▲ Make a red and blue top. What colour is it when you spin it?

▲ Try tops of other colours.

▲ ESSENTIALS FOR SCIENCE: Light and colour

▲ Name _____

Changing colours

You will need: a pencil; coloured Cellophane or a coloured transparent sweet wrapper.

▲ Look through your coloured paper at different objects. How does it change their colours?

I used _____ paper

	Real colour of object	Colour through paper
Sky		
Flower		
Grass		
Pencil		
Brick		

▲ Make some more charts like this. Use different coloured papers.

▲ ESSENTIALS FOR SCIENCE: Light and colour

▲ Name _____

Unmixing colours

You will need: a pencil; paper towels; scissors; a plastic box; bulldog clips; felt-tipped pens; dowling; water.

Some colours are not what they seem.

▲ Cut strips of paper towel.

▲ Draw a line of a different colour across each strip.

▲ Stand them in a little water as shown below. What do you see?

▲ Are Smarties the colours they seem to be? Find out.

▲ ESSENTIALS FOR SCIENCE: Light and colour

▲ Name _____

Rainbows

You will need: a pencil; coloured pencils; felt-tipped pens or crayons.

▲ Colour in the rainbow. Use the correct colours.

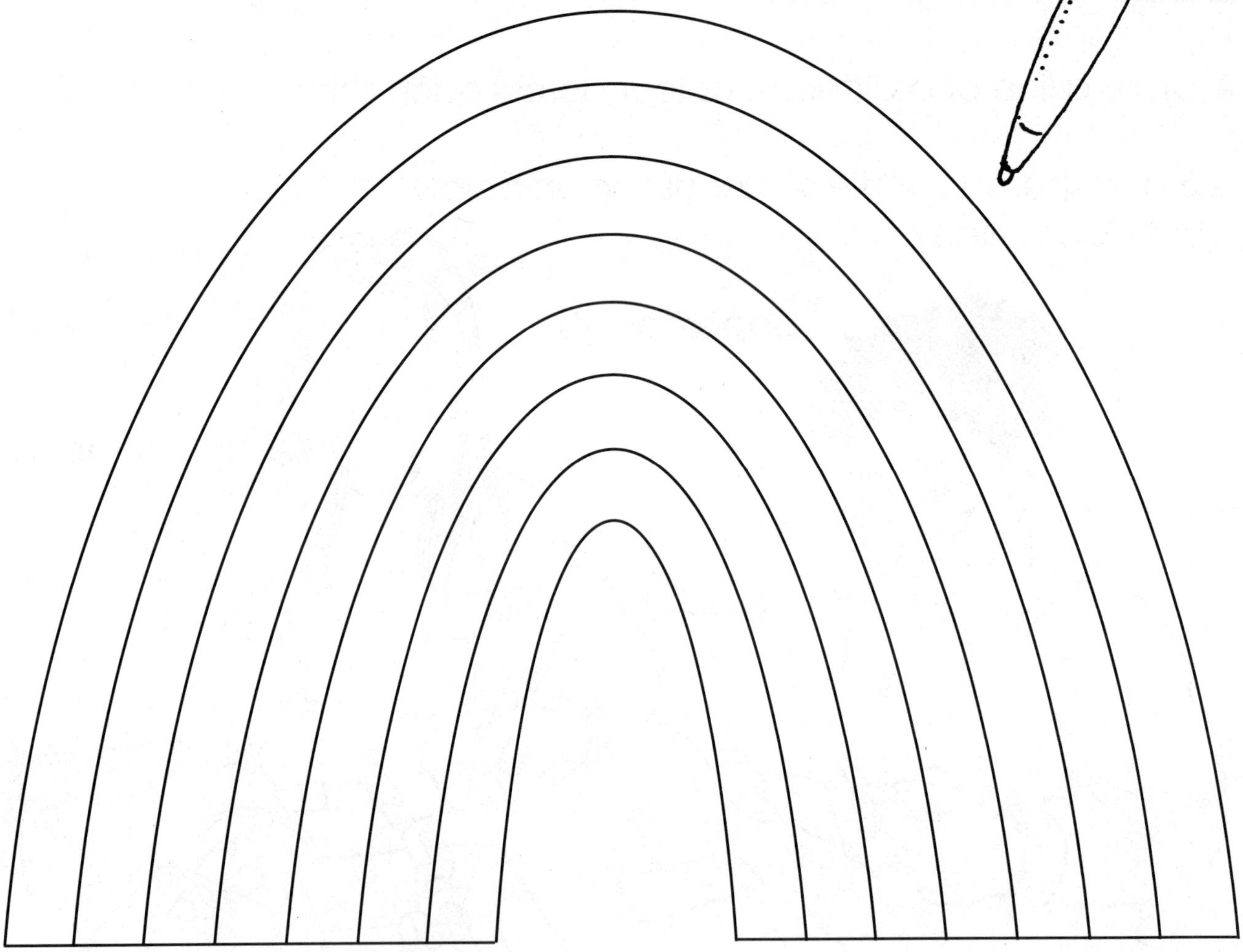

▲ Write down the names of the colours.

_____

_____

_____

▲ Where else have you seen rainbow colours?

▲ ESSENTIALS FOR SCIENCE: Light and colour

▲ Name _____

Shiny things

You will need: a pencil.

▲ Make a collection of shiny things. Light bounces off these things. We say they **reflect** light.

▲ Look at your collection carefully. In which ones can you see your face?

▲ Look at the picture below carefully.
   • Put a tick against the objects you think are shiny.
   • Which of them do you think you could see your face in?

▲ ESSENTIALS FOR SCIENCE: Light and colour

▲ Name _____

Reflections

You will need: a pencil; a large shiny metal spoon.

The picture you see in a mirror is called a **reflection**.

▲ Look at your face in the **front** of the spoon. Draw your reflection below.

▲ Look at your face in the **back** of the spoon. Draw your reflection below.

▲ What do you notice?
▲ Look around your home or school. What other objects make funny reflections?

▲ ESSENTIALS FOR SCIENCE: Light and colour

▲ Name _____

Pictures in the mirror

You will need: a mirror; a pencil.

▲ Use your mirror to see the whole picture. Then draw in the missing half.

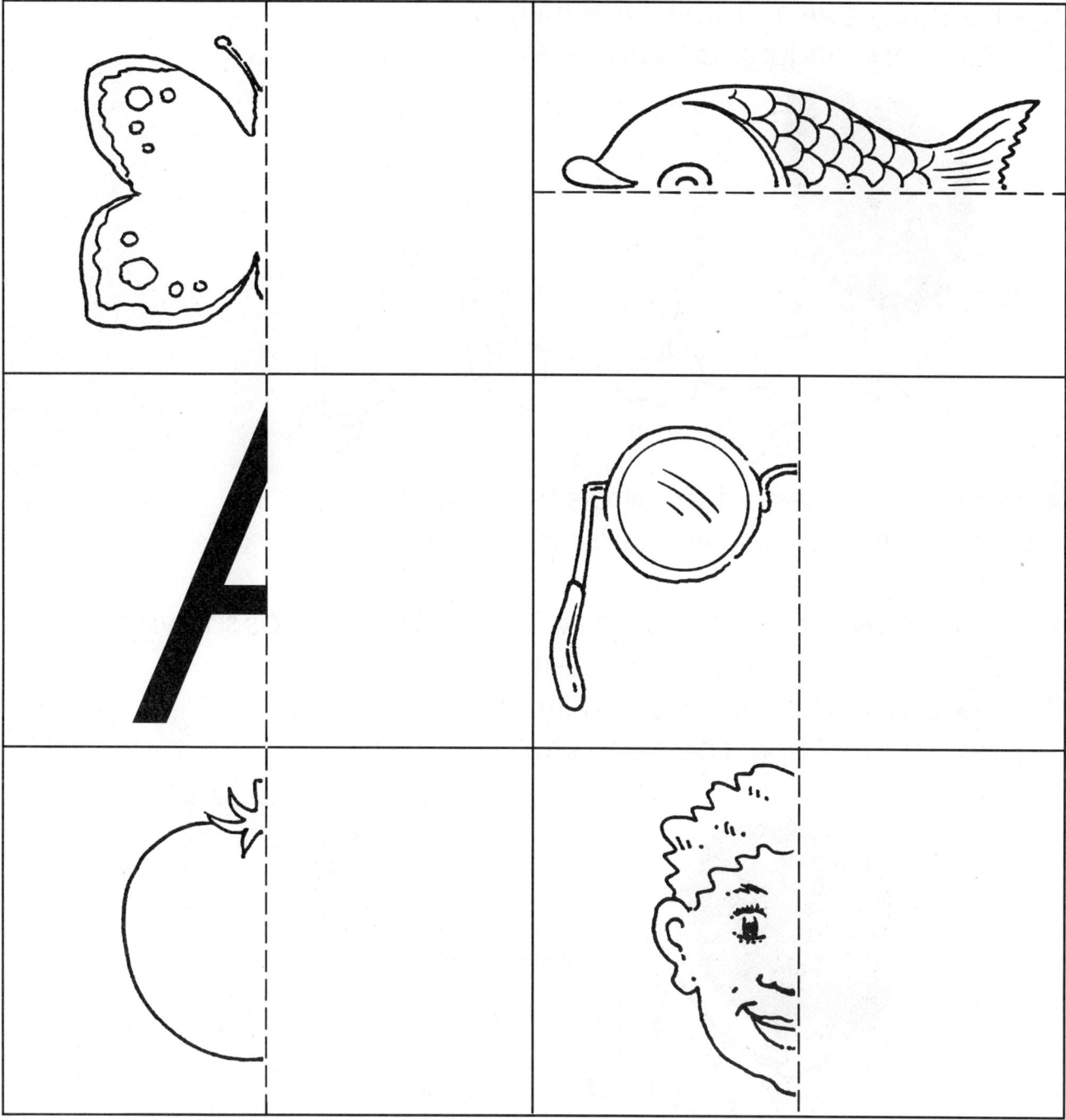

▲ Draw some half pictures of your own. Ask a friend to use a mirror to finish them.

▲ ESSENTIALS FOR SCIENCE: Light and colour

Mirror tricks

You will need: a pencil; two mirrors; sticky tape; Plasticine; a toy figure.

▲ Use sticky tape to join the two mirrors at the back. Stand them as shown below.
  • Put the figure in front of the mirrors.
  • How many figures do you see?

▲ Move the edges of the mirrors towards you.
How many figures can you see now?

▲ Put the two mirrors so that they face each other as shown below.
  • Put the figure in between them.
  • Peep over the top of one mirror into the other.
  • How many figures can you see?

▲ Where in the street or in shops have you seen mirrors being used?

▲ ESSENTIALS FOR SCIENCE: Light and colour

▲ Name _____

Reflecting sunlight

You will need: a pencil; a small mirror.

Do this activity on a sunny day. Do not look at the Sun or shine light in anyone's eyes or on to fabric or paper.

A mirror will reflect the Sun's light.
▲ Use your mirror to make a spot of sunlight shine on a wall.
 • What shape is the spot?
 • Can you make your spot of sunlight move round the room?
 • Can you use your mirror to make the spot of sunlight go round a corner?

▲ ESSENTIALS FOR SCIENCE: Light and colour   27

▲ Name _____

Bending light

You will need: a pencil; a clear beaker of water; a drinking straw; a ruler.

▲ Put the drinking straw in the beaker of water.

• Draw it from the side.   • Draw it from above.

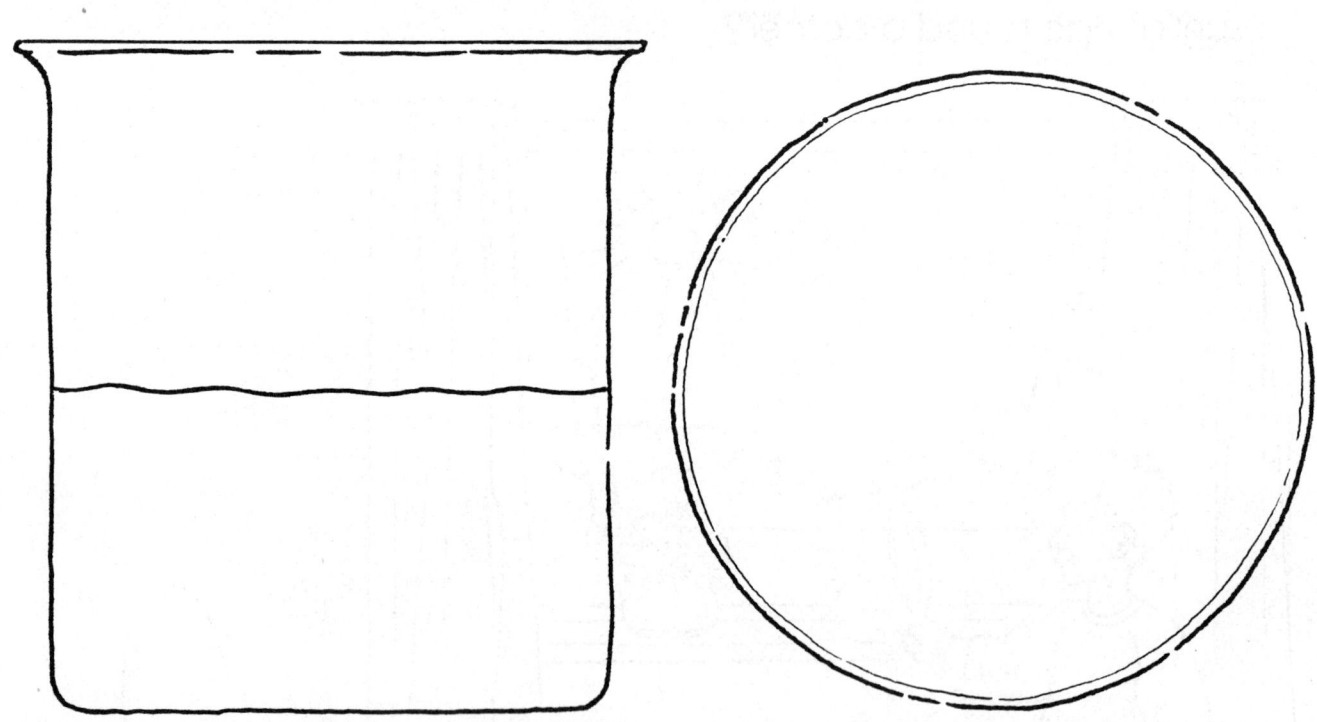

▲ What has happened?

▲ Does the same thing happen to a ruler? Try other objects.

▲ ESSENTIALS FOR SCIENCE: Light and colour   28

▲ Name _____

Magnifying glasses

You will need: a pencil; a magnifying glass; a book.

▲ Look at a book through the magnifying glass.
Do the words look larger or smaller?

▲ What things have magnifying glasses or lenses in them?

▲ Draw some of them below.

▲ ESSENTIALS FOR SCIENCE: Light and colour

▲ Name _____

Make a magnifier

You will need: a clear plastic lid; a wax crayon; a dropping pipette or a drinking straw; a clear jar with a lid.

▲ With the wax crayon draw a small circle in the middle of the lid.

▲ Put one drop of water inside the circle. You have made a magnifier.

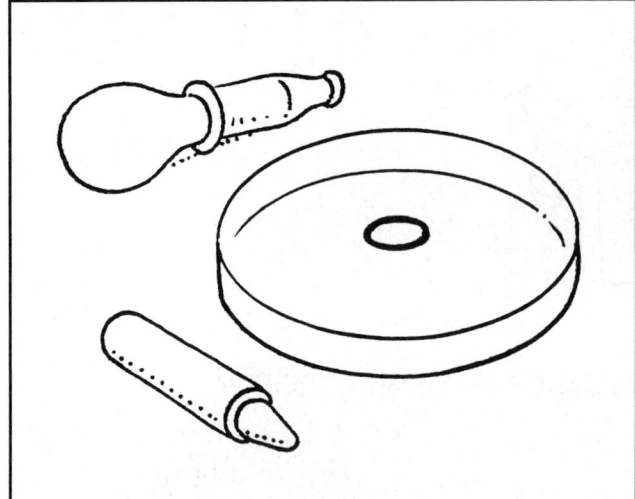
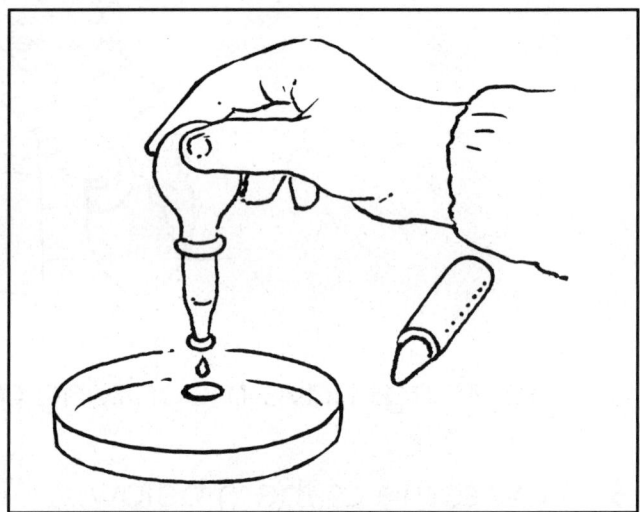

▲ Use your magnifier to look at tiny things

▲ Draw something magnified below.

▲ Fill a clear jar to the top with water. Put the lid on tightly.
  • Can you make the jar of water magnify things?
  • Which way do you have to hold it to make it work best?

▲ ESSENTIALS FOR SCIENCE: Light and colour

▲ Name _____

Animals in the light and dark

You will need: a pencil; a shallow tray; damp paper towels; clear plastic sheet; black card; ten woodlice; a plastic spoon; a paintbrush.

▲ Put damp paper towels in the bottom of a shallow tray.

▲ Place the woodlice in the centre of the tray. Cover the tray as shown in the picture below.

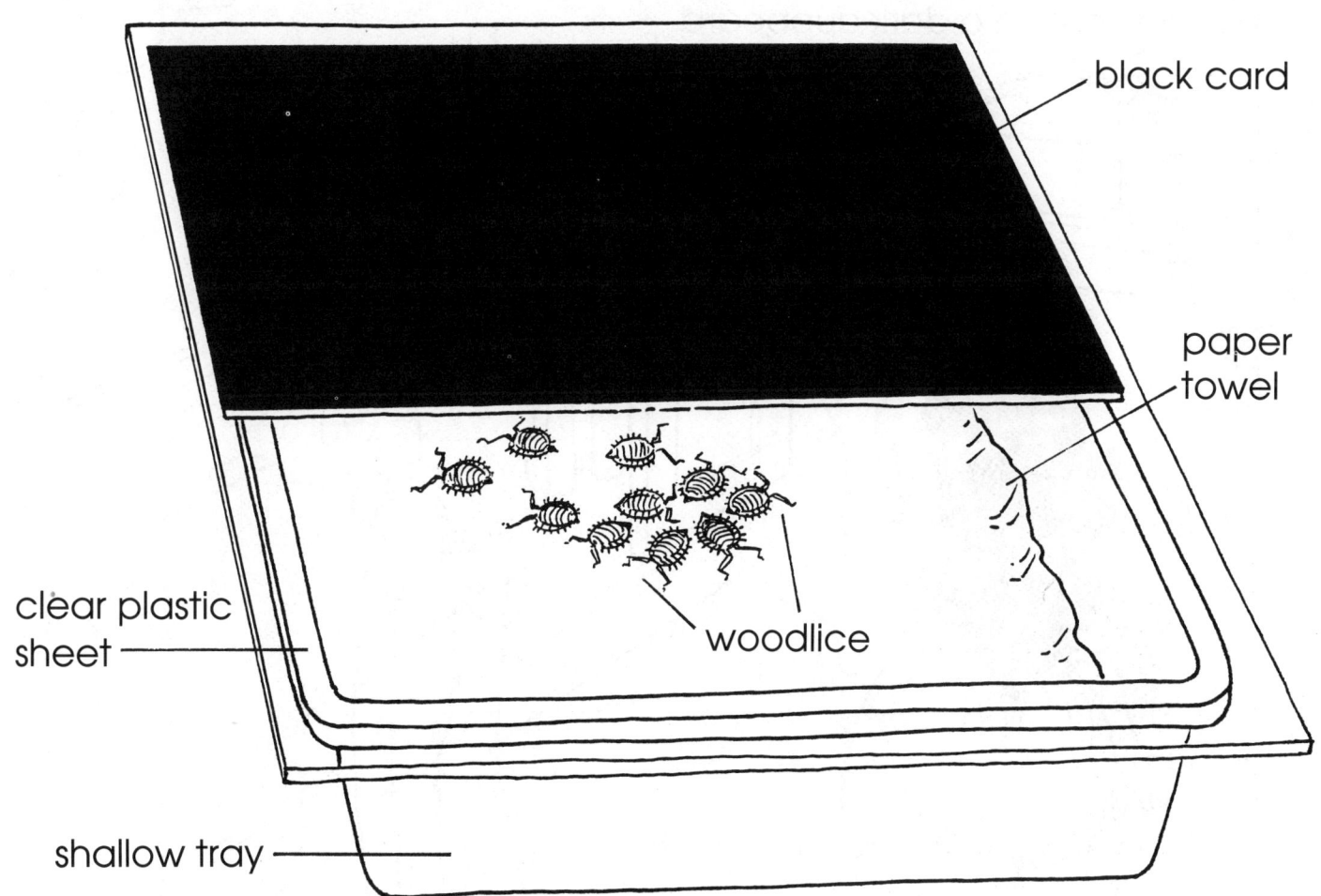

▲ Leave the tray in a light place. Look at it fifteen minutes later.
  • Where are the woodlice?
  • Are they in the light or in the dark?

▲ Which do earthworms like best, light or dark?

▲ ESSENTIALS FOR SCIENCE: Light and colour

▲ Name _____

Plants and light

You will need: a pencil; two saucers; cotton wool or paper towels; cress seeds or grass seeds.

▲ Line the two saucers with wet cotton wool or paper towels.

▲ Sprinkle seeds on both saucers.

▲ Put one saucer on a sunny window-sill. Put the other in a dark cupboard.

▲ Do both lots of seedlings look the same? What happened? Why?

▲ What happens if you put the pot from the dark on the window-sill?

▲ ESSENTIALS FOR SCIENCE: Light and colour